uroboros

Tabetha Moon House

Wider Perspectives Publishing ✕ 2022 ✕ Hampton Roads, Va.

Illustrations by Christine Byrne

© December 2022, Tabetha Moon House, Norfolk, VA.
Tabetha M. House, Tab House and Moon House Healing are related concepts and brands with the author.
Wider Perspectives Publishing, Hampton Roads
ISBN 978-1-952773-68-6

Dedication

This is for
HUMANITY

Intention

Hi soul friend, my heart is full of gratitude that you have chosen my book to read! Ouroboros is my interpretation of life being a challenging, transformative, and beautiful experience that includes infinite endings and beginnings. I see this as a representation of how we are all connected. As humans, we have the capability to feel many emotions. There is a sense of empowerment when we take the time to navigate these emotions and accept the energetic feelings they hold. As you read these poems, my intention is to have a positive influence on feeling your emotions while uncovering your own story. Thank you for being a part of this journey with me, and I hope to connect with you through peace and love.

To marybelle with the beautiful smile and beautiful heart,

Thank you for inspiring me to live with open arms & to enjoy the moments this life offers. I hope you enjoy these poems!

I love you,

♡

Acknowledgment

Kasey and Donovan Dargert
and
Angela and John Beegle

for showing me
unconditional love,
while inspiring me to be my authentic self.

Contents

Timing

The right words,
will be heard,
by the right ears,
when it's their turn.
I have a lot to say,
and I want to be heard.

Breaking,
uncovering,
understanding,
discovery.
Silence,
feeling,
patience,
healing.

Simply being.

Let them be ready,
for all my words.

Breaking

Tabetha House

Weak

My chest is so heavy,
my legs can't hold it up anymore.
The bathroom floor is inviting.
My throat gets tight,
I'm tired of trying.
My heart starts pounding.
I keep thinking about when we were
falling,

then flying!

My wings were snapped.
I look up with fear in my eyes,
confusion on my face.
Now I'm lying on the cold floor,
dying.

Heart Break

You told me you'd never leave me.
You watered me and nourished my core.
You watched me blossom into this young woman,
radiating life to then cut me right at the roots.

I'm in a drought now.

Everything that I look forward to just can't compare
to the path I saw myself on with you.
We had a forest full of dreams.
We created trails together that made it all appear to be the right
route.
You held my hand while breezing through these trails.
Wrapped me in your arms when it got cold,
and let me dance when the sun rose.
The forest was set on fire for you though.
While I was singing,
you were silently screaming.

Why didn't you yell!

Why did you lead me to the blazes?
To then turn and run as soon as we got there.

The forest is gone.
Ashes on the ground.
Sitting in this drought.

I know rain is coming and will shower me.
The sun will shine with its rainbow,
and I will bloom again.

Cruel

It's quite scary being vulnerable.
I want a love that is uncontrollable!
Remember when walls were down,
I didn't feel like a burden to be around.

I realized I was only *tolerable.*

I thought you understood me, and
all of my complexities.
Did something change,
or get rearranged?
I think I was tricked.
Nothing was the same.

Heartbreak changed my space,
filled me,
and took my shape.

I truly am strong.
My heart is a muscle,
but I'm still fragile.
When you decided to break me,
you could have been mindful.
Instead, you were so casual.

Ouroboros

Guilt

It doesn't seem fair.
How do I get to have this life?
Breathing in all this air,
singing in the shower,
dancing every hour,
& you…

don't.

We come from the same family.
Kind of,
except,
I wasn't abandoned
and abused.

I just watched.
I was so little,
so confused.
"This isn't right"

Maybe I can do something!
Let me hug you tight.
When you can't sleep,
come snuggle with me,
in the middle of the night.

I promise I'll keep you safe.
As long as you stay with me.

Please stay with me.

I wish my words could penetrate,
your anger and hate.
I'd be raging too, if I were you.

How do I fix this?
I wish I could.
You know I would!

I'm sorry I couldn't save you.

Running Away

The ocean floor,
calls my name.
I belong there.
I can get through
the crashing waves.

Go ahead lungs,
fill up with salty water.
It won't burn as much
as this air.
It is contaminated.
Lies and deception,
            affection,
                    then rejection.

I'm too much on land.

Please swallow me whole.
I'll learn how to survive,
then live again.

The ocean floor is my home now.
Let me leave this place,
no one will find me.

Drowning

Feeling lost...
lost in all these emotions,
and all of these thoughts.

Feeling like my past
is trying to hold me back.
When really, I've already broken through
the ceiling of glass.
Trying to move forward,
without being so damn sad.

Getting twisted in the fear of love...
more so of being loved.
I don't want to pull you under my current,
please keep your head above.

This soul dives right into the deep end, and
you say you know how to swim?
Well, I'm not even sure
where my ocean begins.
How could you survive my waves
as they crash and bend?
I can promise you
I will hold your hand.
Just don't trust me
to bring you to land.

Ouroboros

Tabetha House

Tired

What if I just let go?
I could let this sorrow
take over my body,
and eat my mind.
There's a war in here,
and I am honestly
tired of trying.

Happiness is a choice,
and dammit,
it's getting harder to choose.
When I wake up,
I think of what I have to lose.

Who would actually notice?
Would I actually be missed?
If I were to disappear,
there wouldn't even be
a goodbye kiss.

Silent Pain

I wear my heart on my sleeve.
I want everyone to see, just how much I bleed.

This blood drips while I rip.
Puddle forming
      on the ground.
I'm not even
      making a sound.
Muffling the pain,
      no words allowed.
Keeping that smile,
      you won't see me frown.
Slowly sinking
      all the way down.

Watch it.
See it.
Don't touch it or feel it.
Silent pain through my veins.
I should come with a warning chain.

Disclosed and exposed.
Never discussed, no way to dispose.

So I wear it every day.

Maybe if you could see that I'm a human too.
We all hurt, and we bleed.
We could connect our broken piece.
Let's become whole and create peace.

Full Circle

Here's a mirror,.
look straight.
Childhood trauma,
that never dissipates.
The pain is so heavy,
you carry all that weight.
Do you see it in your eyes?
You wear it when you rage.

Over the years,
taught how to hate.
A little boy,
so small,
probably eight.
What did you see?
Learning ugly traits.
You couldn't control,
those slaps across her face.

Pause, wait.
I never thought,
we would relate.

Understanding

Tabetha House

Divinity

How did I get to survive?
A world full of abuse and hate,
without being victimized.

I'm on my own timeline.

Somehow escaping
the predator's ties.
I know I've been watched,
seen with their eyes.
When it gets close to my time,
my hands are grabbed.

I am saved,
steered to a new path.

Ouroboros

No Goodbye

There was this one moment in time,
when you were completely mine.
Our stars were perfectly synchronized.

You held the keys to our infinity.
What a beautiful journey we had,
everything was new and nothing was on repeat.

Sometimes I wonder
are you still alive?
You held onto so much of my heart
without paying a single dime.
Oh don't worry now, you don't need to apologize.
Your words would never suffice or justify.

I now know
you didn't see me as the treasured prize.
My rose-colored glasses
made me convenient for you to utilize.
It took me some time,
but I am so happy to realize,
                with my real eyes,
that you were a monster in disguise.

You left without a farewell.
There was no clear reason,
there were no broken spells.
Your heart was cold,
and I thought it would melt.

Reflection brought great clarity.
It's refreshing to see who you are, so clearly.
I forgive you without that apology.

The pain forced me to awaken my eyes.
I can now take in life's beautiful journey,
without being color blind.

Ouroboros

What If

Divine time.
I see the signs.
There was a reason,
our paths aligned.

Your heart is good,
I feel the sweetness.
Something is dark,
you are not fine.

What could you do to me?
Do I even want to know?
I'll think,
"what if"
and have to let it go.

What if it's not the right time?
You weren't a mistake.
There is something more
probably just a lesson I need to learn...

I hope I already learned.

Past Life

My eyes met yours,
I instantly knew.
I've seen you before.
This is deja vu.

Not a familiar face,
it's not your grin.
You take me to a happy place,
to all the lives we were in.

My soul has memories.
What will begin?
We can't go back.
Which life are we in?

Too many questions.
How long has it been?
Maybe before,
we were a sin.

Not this time,
it won't happen again.
What a good moment it was,
when we were more than friends.

Thinking

My heart needs
peace and space.
It gets difficult
to meditate,
when my mind won't
take a break.
All I can think about,
is your embrace.

This doesn't make sense,
it's only been 30 days.

My mind's not straight,
it's all so wrong.
What energy am I feeling?
To know this strong.
There is some reason,
you've sparked my heart.
There must be a meaning.

I'm thinking too hard.

Nothing here is as it seems,
that's what they say.
Life is a backwards game,
I never signed up to play.

You Decide

Isn't she beautiful?
Her water falling so politely.
She is graceful in her essence of power.

Do you think she is majestic?
Do you think she is psychotic?

To me, she flows with grace.
Yet so much *power.*

Is she resilient, or is she determined?
Giving herself to the inevitable.

You have to choose which way to flood.
Some may choose to flood in fear,
she chooses to flood in love.

Invisible

I see you.
Do you see me?
    Are you watching?
        What do I even mean?

Feeling mystical as a mermaid,
boundless and exotic.
A rare breed.
As big as this ocean,
crashing waves,
and a floor so deep.
Are your eyes open?
    Am I just the breeze?
Passing by.
A thought that doesn't even,
cross your mind.
No eyes can see.
Do I even have a purpose?
    How many times will I resurface?

A million.

Just like the waves.
The moon brings in my tide,
always on the right time.

One day you will see me.
I'll be here,
swimming free.

Tabetha House

Be You

When I am completely me,
I feel so free!

and misunderstood.

Who could know someone,
like I wish they could?

I'm still trying to learn my own-self.
I grow bigger and bigger,
while the world shrinks.

Empathy is a trigger.

The more I feel,
the less they can deal.
Aren't we all just trying to heal?

Being alone is inviting,
          kind of exciting,
              and a little despising.
I take myself away from the judgment,
and I fill myself with enlightenment.
I feel so free!

Then the eyes reappear,
and I disappear.

Ouroboros

Dynamic

I know I can be difficult, but
you know I'm worth the trouble.
Can you stand on this shaky ground?
Are you able to understand the rumbles,
as what we once knew crumbles?
Because, after the initial tumble,
we can claim our new land.

I want to love you
        so freely.
I want to see your big smile,
          all cheeky.
I want to let go of resistance,
           forget the whole feeling.
I can hold space for you,
            in all the ways you made need me.

As long as you let me be
authentically me.
Accepting all my complexities,
while knowing the gem inside is a rarity.

Here's the fair warning:
Being true to who I am comes with
never ending learning.
Stay open to the idea that
I am a woman who is forever evolving.

Patience goes a long way
with partnership and some grace.
I promise you that if you stay,
our new world will be full of color,
even on the shaky days.

Not Over

The little boy, just two years old.
He never could imagine what his life would hold.
Never a mistake, or a forgotten case.
He didn't get to choose this life.
It's called fate,
I think?

What a star in all our eyes.
Spiraling that football, when he was only five.

Maybe there was too much
expectation
        or glorification?
Too much pressure.
        Whose dream were we chasing?

No one knew how to handle
his situation.
Lying about
his identification.
I knew this would end
in some sort of devastation.

No.

The story doesn't have to end.
You can change the course of this ramification.

These are your choices now; you get to choose.
Leave this place, leave this town.
I'm telling you, there is nothing left to lose.

No Conditions

My love for you is unconditional.
There is nothing you can do
that will dissolve this love.
You may say I'm just emotional, but
the love I have for you,

it's uncontrollable.

There are no bounds.
This love is free and never ending.
You might not understand it now, but
you can feel it.
Like when you're lost
and need to be found.
My love is there.

I see you.
My love is never hiding.
It may seem distorted,
like when we are fighting.
Underneath all that chaos,
it's more than trying.
My love is a warrior.
I see every piece of you.

I hope you find peace with me.

Remember when you were little,
and would come sleep with me?
I'll always have space for you,
and wrap you in my arms.
I hope my love feels like home
and for the rest of your life,
you know that you are not alone.

Mind Vs. Heart

I don't want you to die.
There's so much more than cancer inside.
You have a light that radiates this world!
How could it go away and make everything
swirl,

      and twirl,

          and curl.

I'm lying in my bed,
paralyzed in my head,
thinking of you dead.

No.

This is my mind trying to scare my heart.
This brain will start,
with its morphed thoughts.
I'm better than being unconscious, because
I know that even when we are apart,
there's no way that we aren't together.

You're in me like a seed.
Your blood flows through my veins.
I look at my face in the mirror,
and I see your eyes,
even through this pain.

I place my hands on my chest,
and it's so warm.
Your love fills me.

Tabetha House

Patience

I don't know what's coming my way.
I do know it's time for me to be still,
and to stay.

I don't do this often,
but I think I'm supposed to pray.
When I do,
God tells me
it's going to be okay.

So I wait.

I'm patient.

What is this for?
So many things keep happening, like
something is trying to bust through my door.
I'm confused, and
I don't know what to think anymore.

It's kind of scary and I don't know why.
I know the universe has got me,
there's no reason to cry.

Ouroboros

Full Circle

Watching abuse,
that we didn't choose.
Powerless,
  emptiness,
    hopelessness,
      and brokenness.
So much yelling,
black outs,
then sharp punches.
Tears of fear,
hiding and realizing,
that no one cares.

There it is again,
more that we both share.

The depth of
how much we care.
It's so intense.
You hold on to me so tight.

It's starting to make sense.

Do you know how to love?
In a nourishing way.
Something gentle,
sweet, and easy.
Are you scared I won't stay?

Your love squeezes me,
ouch, you're holding on so tight.
If I'm not in your control,
flashbacks of those nights.

Healing

Moon Rise

Watching the moon rise,
clears my mind.
She loves to,
bring in my tide.
Reminds me that
I am made of water.
Now,
        I'm healing fine.

She shimmers the ocean,
glimmering like sparkles.
I thought those were my tears,
suddenly, I've lost them.
The moon has stolen my fears,
snatched them and tossed them.
She whispers to me,

"My dear,
I have always been here.
I will stay so near
in all of your years"

She never leaves for long.
Even when you can't see her,
she'll be singing your song.

Mine starts with being heard.
I yell it out loud.
She hears every word.

Realization

I want to say thank you.
You don't even know what you've done.
You showed a girl that she could be so many parts,
and still remain one.

You called me a "firework".
Not even to realize,
you lit the spark.
It was something in your eyes,
allowing me to shine.

You were my catalyst,
with such ease.
You gave me confidence,
and a sense of peace.

I'm coming to realize,
you were never mine.
Not meant to, or,
supposed to be.
Never to cross the line.

I'll keep the sparkle in my heart.
You helped me find the parts of me
that must have gotten lost in the dark.

Thank you for showing me
some people still care.
Even just for a moment to be
special and rare.

Found

You grabbed my hands.
Actually, you held them.
Pulling me up.
You weren't going to let me go down,
never allowing me to drown.

I didn't know how broken I was.
Neither did you.
But because of you,
I survived.
Actually,

I lived.

I'm back home,
and I don't feel so alone.
Even when I'm by myself.
I'm not sure how you did it,

I'm so glad you did.

Now I'm floating.
Sometimes, I get so high,
it can be scary.

You bring me back to the ground,
without trying to shrink me.
All I want is to be found,
and you see me.

Beginnings

What's your vibe?
Roll the windows down,
and just ride.
Don't worry about the time.
Keep your eyes open,
you'll see the signs.
Just keep driving
life is so divine.

Let the sun touch your skin.
Take your hair down,
let it blow in the wind.
The smell of a new day,
choose anything.

Let life begin.

Unity

I'm not surviving,
I'm living.
That includes,
a lot of feeling,
heart break,
then healing.

Over and over,
and over again.

I'd rather that,
than blindly being.
I'm in love with

leading,
seeing,
dreaming!

It is incredibly freeing.

Life can be devastating.
When we uplift others,
we are not debilitated.
The world feels less
separated.

We are more connected.

Frequency

Living this life
    with no hesitation.
Not worried about
    any expectation.
We are all connected
    through the vibration.
Source guiding us
    to the manifestation.
Blessed to have
    this realization.

We are all made up of
    endless love.

Every morning
love is pouring.
Always free,
just feel
your heart beat.

Community

This is connection,
I feel what it means.
No words are needed,
we just feel that beat.

Together through
love,
joy,
and soul.
What a magical moment.
My heart is graciously full.

Stepping to our own beat,
making up the hums.
Letting the rhythm guide us,
flowing through our thumbs.
No language to speak of,
keep the words on my tongue.
Vibrations flow through my body.
Can you feel the drums?

Close your eyes.
Feel the sunlight
kiss your mind.
What a blissful moment.
Push pause on time.

Just Right

Play in my waters,
I keep it just the right feeling of warm.
Bring all your friends,
we will be reborn.

It's fluid and easy,
there are only little waves.
There are mermaids and starfish.
Everyone is saved.

We stay safe here.
I'll hold your hands.
Run my fingers in your hair,
while we lay in the sand.

If the water gets rocky,
like sometimes it can.
You won't go alone.
Our feet will touch land.

Ouroboros

Ease

We float here.
We stay sincere.
Why so much fear?
We will make it my dear.
We are endless,
           timeless,
                  priceless,
                        and if we rewind this,
it will stay so clear.
We will keep floating,
year after year.

Friendship

When I think of a beautiful friendship,
my mind goes to the beach.

We were in Williamsburg,
laughing until our bellies hurt.
A day that was so perfect,
without even a word.

I never knew how much I needed you.
Your heart heard.

That's the beauty, you see.
We didn't even have to try.
I was meant to be your best friend,
and you were meant to be mine.

Peace

Do you notice how the sun paints the sky?

Every single day.
Never late,
and never early,

always on time.

Most days orange,
some days are pink.

I get mesmerized on my ride.

Love

The moon is out tonight.
She's huge and radiating light.

I love how she speaks to me,
whispers to my soul.

Looking at her during the night,
feels like I'll never get old.

Serenity

What a sweet treat.

Driving quietly,
able to still see your beauty.
You light up the street.

You are so gracious.

Most mornings you have disappeared,
but today you are still here.
Life feels incredibly clear.

Sunset

When the sun says goodbye,
she does it with grace.
Watch the sky,
as she illustrates.
Breathe it all in,
prepare to separate.
Sit in the moment
let your soul meditate.

What a beautiful way,
to end any day.

The dance she does,
has a flow.
Inch by inch,
she takes it slow.
She gives you time
to watch her fall low.
Then all at once,
she has to go.

Dance Floor

We lived forever on that dance floor.
Music lifting our feet.
I was looking at you,
you were looking at me.
Dancing carefree to the beat.

It was like tomorrow would never start.
Jumping to the stars,
where there are no scars.

With eyes so alive,
turquoise and green,
infinity didn't feel so far.

I promise you,
that night will live forever.

Rolling

So many poems,
that keep flowing.
I don't want my mind
to stop growing.
I love this feeling.
I pray to God
please keep the momentum going.

Life feels light,
when I express my words
just right.
Articulation just might
be the key to unlock

infinity.

Thank you, Universe.
Let's keep this on repeat.
My mind never shuts off,
so might as well take a seat,
and rest those feet.
Let my mind
write with a beat

Tingling

I'm floating,
steady flying.
Off to my own universe,
my own skyline.

What world am I in?
No need for time.
Love calling me up,
my vibrations keep rising.

Up in the clouds,
the sky is so blue.
I can see clearer now,
with this bird's eye view.

Everything is starting to make sense.
I think I've found me again!
Tip toeing with that idea,
life feels less tense.

I want to keep floating,
I won't drown.
Letting my soul,
be taken off the ground.

Gratitude

Warmth kissing your skin from the sun.
Moonlight guiding you as the day is done.
Wind blowing between the leaves.
Crisp air entering your nose when you breathe.
Chirping birds when your eyes open.
Long exhales that can make your mind quiet.
Sparkles created from snow being so white.
Crashing waves that are infinite.
Smell of newness that comes after rain.
Gentleness of sand under your feet.
Enormous trees providing shade.
Never ending stars as you gaze.
Fluffy clouds that stir your imagination.

Isn't life a wonderful creation.

Stay

Give me something gentle and sweet.
I want to be wrapped in your arms,
while we intertwine out feet.
Laying beside you,
          behind you,
               inside of you,
We've cultivated this moment of peace.
Hard to describe, but we melt together with an ease.
I've never known or seen.
This feeling of connection, it's all I could ever need.
Is this luck or alignment?
All I can do is stay right in it.
Not wanting to question the situation,
while holding no expectation.
We only need to live in the present.

Let me be your girl.
See the smile in my eyes?
I could light up your world.
Caress you and undress you,
I know what gentle and sweet could be.

Ouroboros

10:10

Now and then.
Save or send.
Straight then bend.
Lover once friend.
Saint vs. sin.
End and begin.

Go again.

10:10

Full Circle

I love you too, please let me go.
You raised a woman well,
let go of your control.
I'm still here,
I'm not running away.

I want to fly!

To let go of this pain.

Don't be so scared,
fear is exhausting.
Please keep breathing.
You haven't lost me.

You never could,
over a thousand lives.
Our connection,
it's special.
It is divine.

We will get through this together,
even when we are separated.
Remember that trauma?
Together we can dissipate it.

Ouroboros

Tabetha House

Alignment

I am back.
Here we are.
Able to breathe.
We've come so far.
The numbers add up.
Healing the scars.

I love you moon,
I love you stars.
I love you sun,
it's not so dark.

God,
Universe,
Source,
Light,
Vibrations,
Frequency,
All is right.

Thank you.
Thank you.
Thank you,
I'll say it a million times.

Then I'll scream,

I love you!

My chest isn't so tight.

Colophon

Brought to you by Wider Perspectives Publishing, care of James Wilson, with the mission of advancing the poetry and creative community of Hampton Roads, Virginia.
This page used to have many cute and poetic expressions, but the sheer number of quality artists deserving mention has superseded the need to art. This has become some serious business; please check out how *They art...*

Travis Hailes- Virgo, thePoet
Nick Marickovich
Grey Hues
Madeline Garcia
Chichi Iwuorie
Symay Rhodes
Tanya Cunningham-Jones
      (Scientific Eve)
Terra Leigh
Raymond M. Simmons
Samantha Borders-Shoemaker
Taz Weysweete'
Jade Leonard
Darean Polk
Bobby K.
      (The Poor Man's Poet)
J. Scott Wilson (TEECH!)
Charles Wilson
Gloria Darlene Mann
Neil Spirtas
Jorge Mendez & JT Williams
Sarah Eileen Williams
Stephanie Diana (Noftz)
Shanya – Lady S.
Jason Brown (Drk Mtr)
Ken Sutton
Crickyt J. Expression
Se'Mon-Michelle Rosser

Lisa M. Kendrick
Cassandra IsFree
Nich (Nicholis Williams)
Samantha Geovjian Clarke
Natalie Morison-Uzzle
Gus Woodward II
Patsy Bickerstaff
Edith Blake
Jack Cassada
Dezz
M. Antoinette Adams
Catherine TL Hodges
Kent Knowlton
Linda Spence-Howard
Tony Broadway
Zach Crowe
Mark Willoughby
Martina Champion
... and others to come soon.

the Hampton Roads
      Artistic Collective
      (757 Perspectives) &
The Poet's Domain
are all WPP literary journals in cooperation with Scientific Eve or Live Wire Press

Check for those artists on FaceBook, Instagram, the Virginia Poetry Online channel on YouTube, and other social media.

Hampton Roads Artistic Collective is an extension of WPP which strives to simultaneously support worthy causes in Hampton Roads and the local creative artists.

Made in the USA
Middletown, DE
19 July 2023

34931161R00047